ROCKET AROUND *Washington DC!*

Written by
**Lee
Lynch**

Illustrations by
**Emma
Lynch**

Contributors
**Jeffrey,
Jack, &
Tom
Lynch**

ROCKET AROUND LLC   U.S.A.

This book is for neurodiverse kids of any age, who love adventure, imagination, and finding new ways to have fun!

Neurodiverse people behave, think, and learn differently from people with neurotypical brains. These differences include strengths. In a word, neurodiverse people are awesome. Neurodiverse people might be autistic, live with ADHD, dyslexia, PTSD, Tourette's, or other things.

Safety Tips

Being safe when you travel is important. Remember to:

-Make sure you can see the adult you're with

-Set a meeting place in case you cannot find your adult

-Know your adult's phone number - write it here:

-If you feel lost, ask a police officer or information person for help

Be Safe!

Everywhere We Go in This Book

Arlington National Cemetery, Pg. 9

The National Mall, Pg. 10

Lincoln Memorial, Pg. 10

Vietnam Memorial, Pg. 11

Korean War Veteran's Memorial, Pg. 11

National World War II Memorial, Pg. 12

The White House, Pg. 13

Washington Monument, Pg. 14

National Museum of American History, Pg. 15

National Children's Museum, Pg. 16

National Archives Building, Pg. 17

National Gallery of Art Sculpture Garden, Pg. 17

National Museum of Natural History, Pg. 18 and 19

Smithsonian 'castle' (Smithsonian Institution Building), Pg. 20

You can also see where all of the above sites are located on the map on Pg. 32

Everywhere We Go continued

Carousel on the Mall, Pg. 20

National Museum of African American History and Culture, Pg. 21

National Portrait Gallery, Pg. 21

National Gallery of Art, Pg. 21

National Air and Space Museum, Pg. 22 and 23

National Museum of the American Indian, Pg. 24

U.S. Botanic Garden, Pg. 24

United States Capitol, Pg. 25

Library of Congress, Pg. 26

National Postal Museum, Pg. 27

International Spy Museum, Pg. 28

Jefferson Memorial, Pg. 29

Tidal Basin, Pg. 29

MLK (Martin Luther King) Memorial, Pg. 29

FDR (Franklin Delano Roosevelt) Memorial, Pg. 29

Memorial Bridge, Pg. 29

See page 43 to be a ROCKETAROUNDER!

Hello human friends!

My name is Rocket the travel pug.

I love to visit cool new places.

Adventure is one of my favorite things (behind humans and sleep).

You too? Great! Let's travel together!

Today my human family is going to the District of Columbia, also known as Washington DC or just DC.

It's the capital of the United States.

I love being at home with my fabulous human family -- Mom, Dad, Jeffrey, Jack, and Emma. Here are their pictures.

But I also LOVE seeing new places.

DC is not far from my house. I just know they are taking me with them!

They wouldn't leave ME behind, right?

They're zipping up their backpacks so we must be leaving.

And they are out the door!

Wait – what about me? They must not know they left me behind.

I'll try the back door...Hi-ya! I am out!!

Now, where did they go?

Sniff, sniff - I smell them! Come with me!

They hopped on the Metro train to go into the city. We will too.

We're probably not supposed to be on here alone, so we'll just hide under this Metro seat.

The train stopped. Sniff, sniff - my humans got off here, at [Arlington National Cemetery](). Since 1864, it's been a cemetery and today it has gravesites for more than 14,000 veterans. There's so much to see here, so it's great that there's a tram that goes all around the cemetery.

Let's go inside. OH NO – NO DOGS ALLOWED!

Sniff, sniff. Smells like my humans are heading this way.

Arlington National Cemetery

What to See

-The graves of American heroes who have served America, such as former Presidents William Howard Taft and John F. Kennedy.

-It also has the Tomb of the Unknown Soldier, which has the remains of unknown soldiers from World War I, World War II, and the Korean War, and a sculpture honoring servicewomen and dogs.

Look for other interesting and fun facts on page 34!

What to See

The words from two of President Lincoln's most famous speeches -- the Gettysburg Address and his address after he was elected a second time – are inscribed on the walls in big letters.

Can you read them out loud? Great job!

They're at the Lincoln Memorial – one of the most beautiful monuments in a city full of monuments!

More than seven million people visit here every year. It sits at one end of what's called the National Mall – a huge open area of memorials, museums, and even pools of water -- stretching to the U.S. Capitol.

Inside, it has a giant statue of Abraham (Abe) Lincoln, the 16th U.S. president who led America through the Civil War. Uh oh – I've lost my humans' scent. Time to move on!

Lincoln Memorial

10

Sniff, sniff. Over here!

They walked through the [Vietnam Veterans Memorial](#).

Then they came over here to the [Korean War Veterans Memorial](#).

These are really cool things, but where are my humans?? Sniff, sniff. They went this way.

Vietnam Veterans Memorial

Korean War Memorial

What to See

The Vietnam Veterans Memorial lists the names of the more than 58,000 Americans who died serving in the Vietnam War (1959-1975).

The Korean War Veterans Memorial is dedicated to the women and men who served in the armed forces during the Korean War (1951 – 1953), including those who died serving.

Are those soldiers looking at you? Go to page 34 to find out.

What to See

The columns stand for the role that U.S. states and territories played in winning the war.

There are two engravings of "Kilroy was here" in the memorial. Kilroy is a doodle that soldiers use to draw on places. Can you find Kilroy on the memorial?

It's the National World War II Memorial, honoring the 16 million people who served America during World War II (1939 – 1945).

It's amazing – 56 columns in a semi-circle around a beautiful fountain and pool (so refreshing). Yikes - I've lost my family's scent! They walked over here.

World War II Memorial

To the White House – where the President and his family live!

Every president has lived and worked here while serving as president since John Adams in 1800.

It's bigger than it looks. It has six stories, 132 rooms, and a huge lawn for the presidential dogs. Lucky pups!

You can go inside for tours, but it smells like my humans have moved on.

What to See

Inside the White House: 35 bathrooms, 28 fireplaces, three elevators, a movie theater, a tennis court, a jogging track, a swimming pool, a putting green.

The White House also has 147 windows - all bulletproof!

A big fire set by British troops damaged a lot of it in 1814, but it's been repaired.

Rocket ar the White House

I think they came over here to the [Washington Monument](#), honoring America's first president, George Washington. It sits at the center of the Mall.

Man is that TALL! It reminds me of one of my other favorite things – a really big stick. If only I could get my mouth around it.

Wait – what am I doing? I need to find my humans. Sniff, sniff - smells like history.

Washington Monument

What to See

The Washington Monument is the tallest building on the National Mall.

Sometimes the elevator inside is open and you can go to the top.

They're in the [National Museum of American History](#)! Finding them in there will be tricky. NO DOGS ALLOWED! Time to get sneaky. I'll get into this kid's backpack and strike my best, stuffed animal pose. I'm in!

Look - it's the original Star-Spangled Banner flag, Abe Lincoln's top hat, and Dorothy's ruby slippers from The Wizard of Oz. There are even video games!

I'll bet my humans are with the video games.

Oh no! I think they've left.

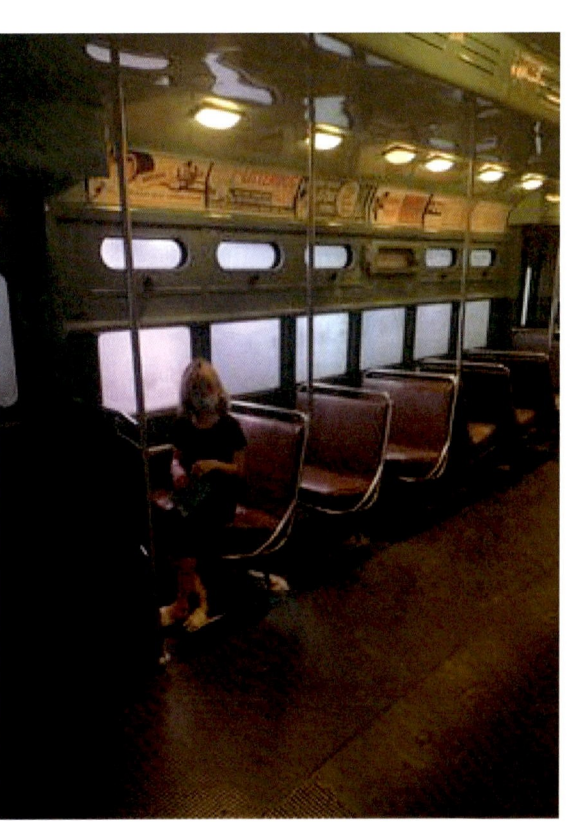

What to See

The first computer bug and an exhibit on how cars, buses, trains, and airplanes helped America grow. Plus there are lots of kids' technology activities.

15

What to See

The National Children's Museum has endless activities: Finding my superpower, practicing baseball hitting and pitching, air basketball, model car racing, a wall to measure how high you can touch while jumping, a craft studio, a giant video screen, and more.

They're here at the [National Children's Museum](#)! Oh brother – there's that sign again – NO DOGS ALLOWED! Time to get sneaky.

I'll climb up this pole, go across the roof, climb onto the ceiling, and go down the three-story slide – WOO HOO!

They have everything here -- climbing contraptions, a giant bubble-making machine, a science alley, virtual games, building blocks. Where do I start! Hold on - Sniff, sniff. I'm losing my humans' scent. Gotta go!

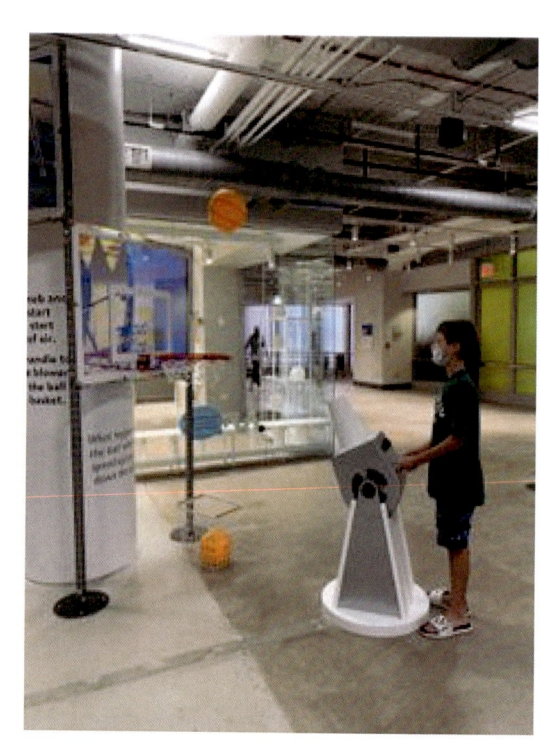

Looks like they're headed toward the [National Archives Building](#), where America's Charters of Freedom – the original Declaration of Independence, U.S. Constitution, and Bill of Rights - are on display.

I can't believe it – NO DOGS ALLOWED! Dog-gone. My humans are on the move. They must be heading through the [National Gallery of Art Sculpture Garden](#). Sniff, sniff. And they are heading on again!

What to See

At the Archives - original papers, letters, and stories of the amendments to the U.S. Constitution, and of the struggles Americans faced to gain rights.

At the Sculpture Garden - six acres of giant modern sculptures – even a giant spider sculpture! In the middle is a fountain that's an ice-skating rink in the winter.

National Archives

Sculpture Garden

17

They went to the National Museum of Natural History. I love that place - so much in there about animals. We'll just head on in - NO DOGS ALLOWED? Are you kidding? If I were stuffed, they'd put me on display!

Time to get sneaky. If I stay low to the ground, I can back in through the exit as people are walking out. Whew! I almost got stepped on. The giant whale and mega-toothed shark display hanging from the ceiling are kind of freaking me out.

I love the dinosaur bones exhibit! How can I take one of those home to bury in my yard? I wonder if they're here in the Human Origins exhibit. Look -- it's a picture on the screen of what Jack would look like as an early human! They've got to be nearby!

National Museum of Natural History

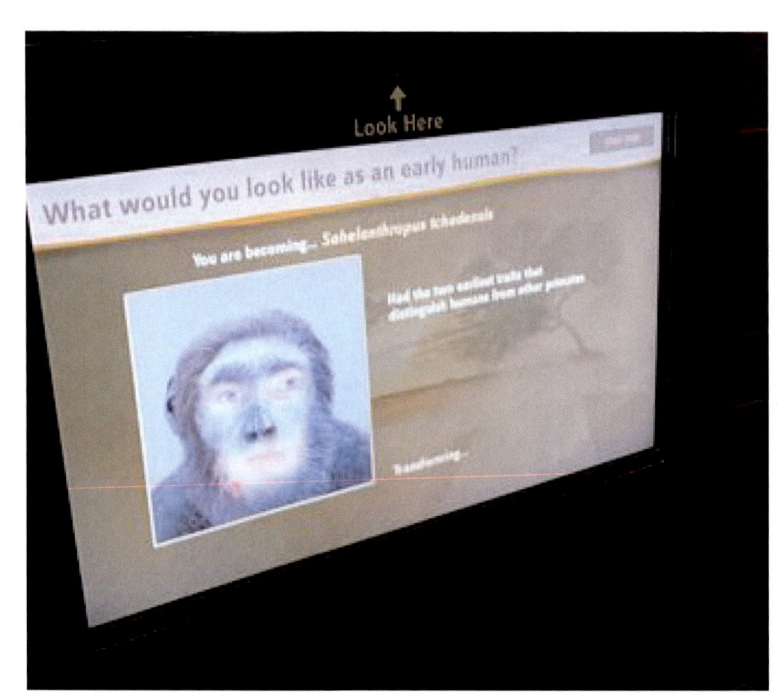

National Museum of Natural History

What to See

The huge stuffed African elephant in the middle is really cool.

And the exhibits are amazing – oceans, mummies from ancient Egypt, mammals – like early and wild dogs (dingos), a butterfly pavilion, a live insect zoo, and gems, minerals, and rocks.

There's even a video game display where you can save the world from a dangerous virus.

What to See

James Smithson (1765-1829) was an English scientist who loved learning and wanted to increase knowledge among humans. He never made it to the U.S., but he left all of his money to create the Smithsonian Institution, which today includes 19 museums, 21 libraries, nine research centers, and a zoo. Most are located in Washington DC and many are free to enter.

There they are - heading out the door and over toward a big red building called the Smithsonian Visitor Center. It's called the castle because it looks like one. Hmmm - it smells like my humans have been on the Carousel on the Mall – all horses except for one sea dragon.

It's the only carousel in Washington DC.

Oh geez – they've moved on.

Smithsonian "Castle"

Carousel

Speaking of Smithsonian museums, my humans headed to the National Museum of African American History and Culture. It's all about African American life, history, and culture.

It's a great place to visit, but my humans have moved on to the National Portrait Gallery and the National Gallery of Art.

Museum of African American History

What to See

The National Portrait Gallery – another Smithsonian museum – has America's only full collection of presidential portraits outside of the White House.

The National Gallery of Art has more than 140,000 pieces of art created over hundreds of years. It might take them a while to get through there. Some of the pieces of art are of dogs, like me!

National Gallery of Art

Now, they're heading to the National Air and Space Museum! And once again NO DOGS ALLOWED. This does not make sense -- my collar tag says ROCKET!!!

Okay, I'll squeeze in between these nice humans and we'll all cruise into the museum together - we're in!

The Smithsonian National Air and Space Museum has the world's largest collection of aviation and space artifacts.

It's one of America's most visited museums.

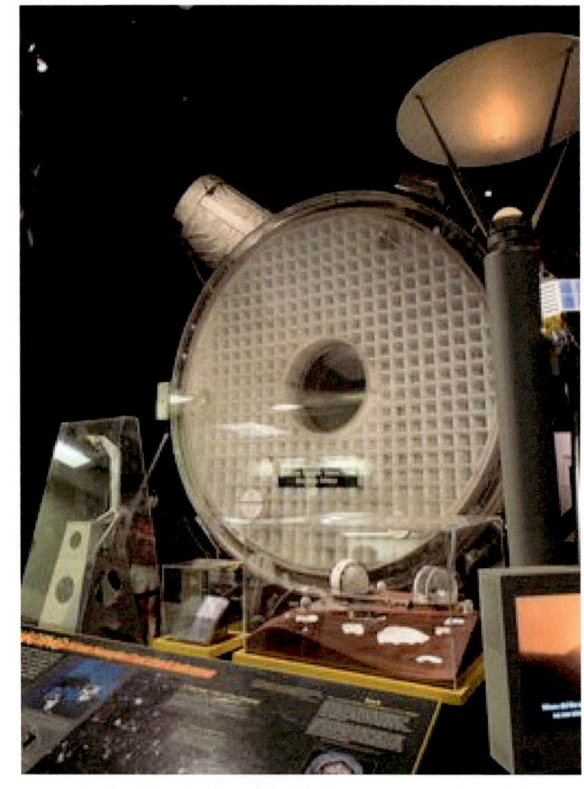

22

They have everything about flight in here.

Sniff, sniff - no idea why my humans are moving on from the Air and Space, but there they go!

National Air and Space Museum

What to See

EVERYTHING! Information about the U.S. space missions to the moon and different planets!

Giant telescopes, astronomy, navigation, and time-keeping devices, plus one of the planes built by the Wright brothers - the first to invent, build, and fly the first airplane with a motor.

So many ROCKETS here!! They even have a statue of Sydney the dog explorer here.

Make sure you fly a rocket simulator while you are here - it goes upside down!

What to See

The National Museum of the American Indian is one of the world's largest collections of Native pieces telling the story of the history and lives of American Indians.

The U.S. Botanic Garden is a living plant museum and the oldest constantly operating botanic garden in the U.S. How many different colors of flowers do you see here?

They went into the National Museum of the American Indian. Can't wait to go inside. Oh no, my humans are moving on!

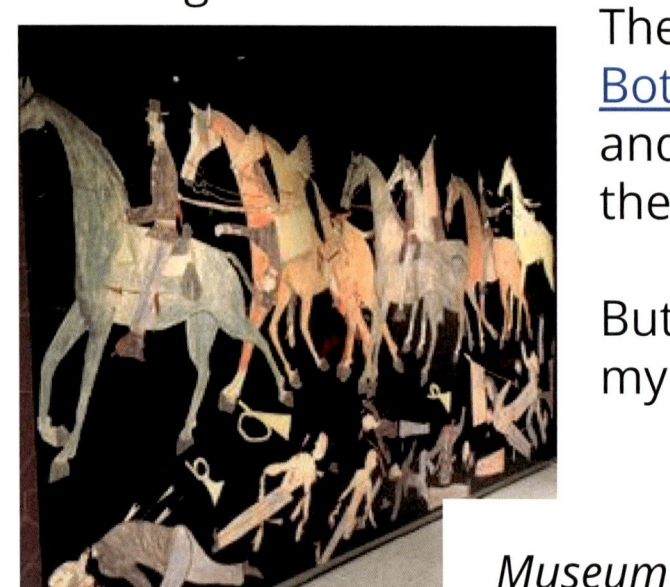

They are heading to the U.S. Botanic Garden. So many plants and flowers - I just love to sniff them all.

But what I do not smell here are my humans.

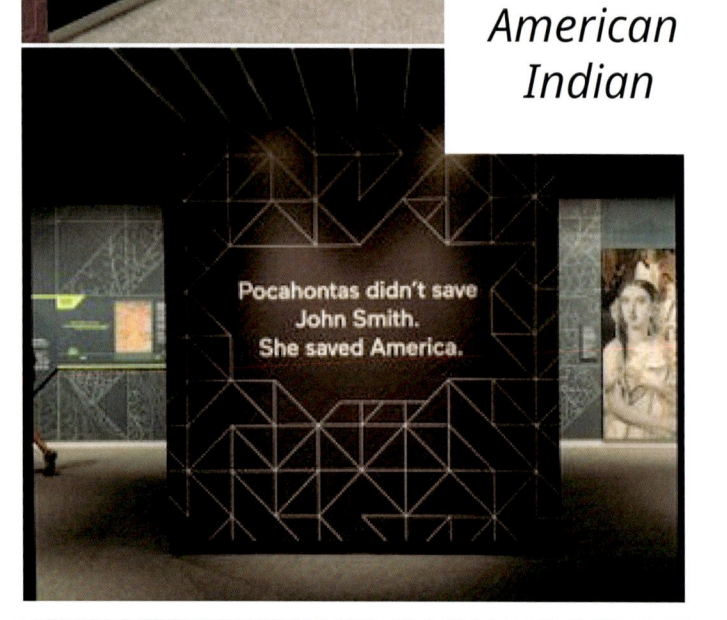

Museum of the American Indian

U.S. Botanical Gardens

24

The U.S. Capitol is right across the street - they must be heading there.

You can't miss it – its dome and the statue of Lady Freedom on top are popular images representing America's democratic form of government.

And it has another refreshing reflecting pool in front of it. Maybe I'll just cool off in there. Oh no – just when things were getting interesting, it smells like my humans have moved on.

U.S. Capitol and reflecting pool

What to See

It's a cool place both because of how it looks and what's usually happening inside.

Since the year 1800, this is where the U.S. Congress meets to discuss the business of the American people.

The dome shape of Statuary Hall creates a sound effect where you can stand yards away and hear someone whispering to you.

Try it!

What to See

Inside are millions of books, photographs, newspapers, and other media and documents. It has the world's largest law library of books, music, and motion pictures. It already has more than 170 million items, and every day it adds another 10,000 pieces. What's your favorite book? Is it in this library?

They went into the Library of Congress – the biggest library in the entire world.

This is where researchers for the U.S. Congress find information.

I hope my humans aren't going to try to read EVERYTHING in here.

Smells like they're heading somewhere else.

26

They went into the [National Postal Museum](#) – the old post office building for the city of Washington DC, turned into amazing displays about postal history and "philately", or the study of postage stamps.

You can do fun things here - even make a virtual collection of dog stamps! My favorite display is of Owney, the Railway Mail Service mascot dog (1887 – 1897) who rode the mail rail cars for most of his life!

Wait - is that my human family back on the bus?! Come on!

What to See

You can design your own stamp, make a "virtual" collection of stamps, and play games where you sort mail packages.

The museum also has different mail delivery machines on display – a horse-drawn carriage, a postal truck, a rail car, airplanes, a huge truck, and even a dog sled!

27

Whew – that bus moves fast! But they got off here, at the [International Spy Museum](), the perfect place for a pup with my sneakiness!

This place is not going to be easy to sneak into. Alright – I'll go up onto the roof, down the air duct, and drop into the car of the world's most famous movie spy, James Bond. YES - I'm in.

What to See

You can get your undercover assignment then do all kinds of super-fun spy activities.

You can see tons of spy gadgets and check out famous spies and their tricks.

You can even try cracking codes.

It's the largest collection on international 'espionage' (fancy word for spying) anywhere in the world. Visiting this place has made me even sneakier! But - Sniff, sniff - my humans are on the move again.

28

Hurry - they're back on the bus! But I'm close behind. There it goes past the Jefferson Memorial, a beautiful dome structure in honor of Thomas Jefferson (1743 – 1826).

But there's no time to stop - the bus is heading past the Martin Luther King Memorial, Franklin Delano Roosevelt Memorial, and the Kennedy Center, and it's going toward Memorial Bridge.

That must mean my human family is heading home! Uh oh – I need to get home fast. My humans will worry if I'm not there.

What to See

In Spring, the more than 3,700 cherry trees around the Jefferson Memorial and Tidal Basin are covered with beautiful white flowers that look like little snowballs.

Clockwise from top: Jefferson Memorial, Tidal Basin, FDR Memorial, MLK Jr. Memorial

The fastest way home is to hop on the Metro, cut through the yards in my neighborhood, scratch on the door, and sneak past the dog walker as she opens it.

Whew – that was close! My humans are so happy to see me but they don't know how lucky they were to have me watching out for them all day!

We had an incredible time rocketing around DC! Thanks for traveling with me.

I don't know about you, but it wore me out.

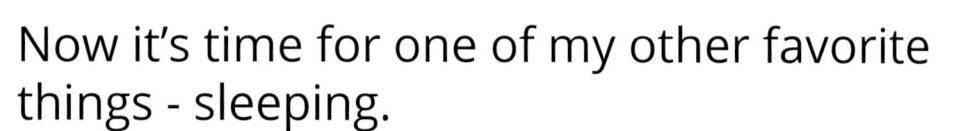

Now it's time for one of my other favorite things - sleeping.

Catch you on our next adventure, after some zzzzzzzzzzzzzzzzzzzzzzzzzzzzzzzzzzzzzz's

ACTIVITY PAGES

FUN!

The National Mall & Downtown Washington DC

Match the numbers to the sites on the next page.

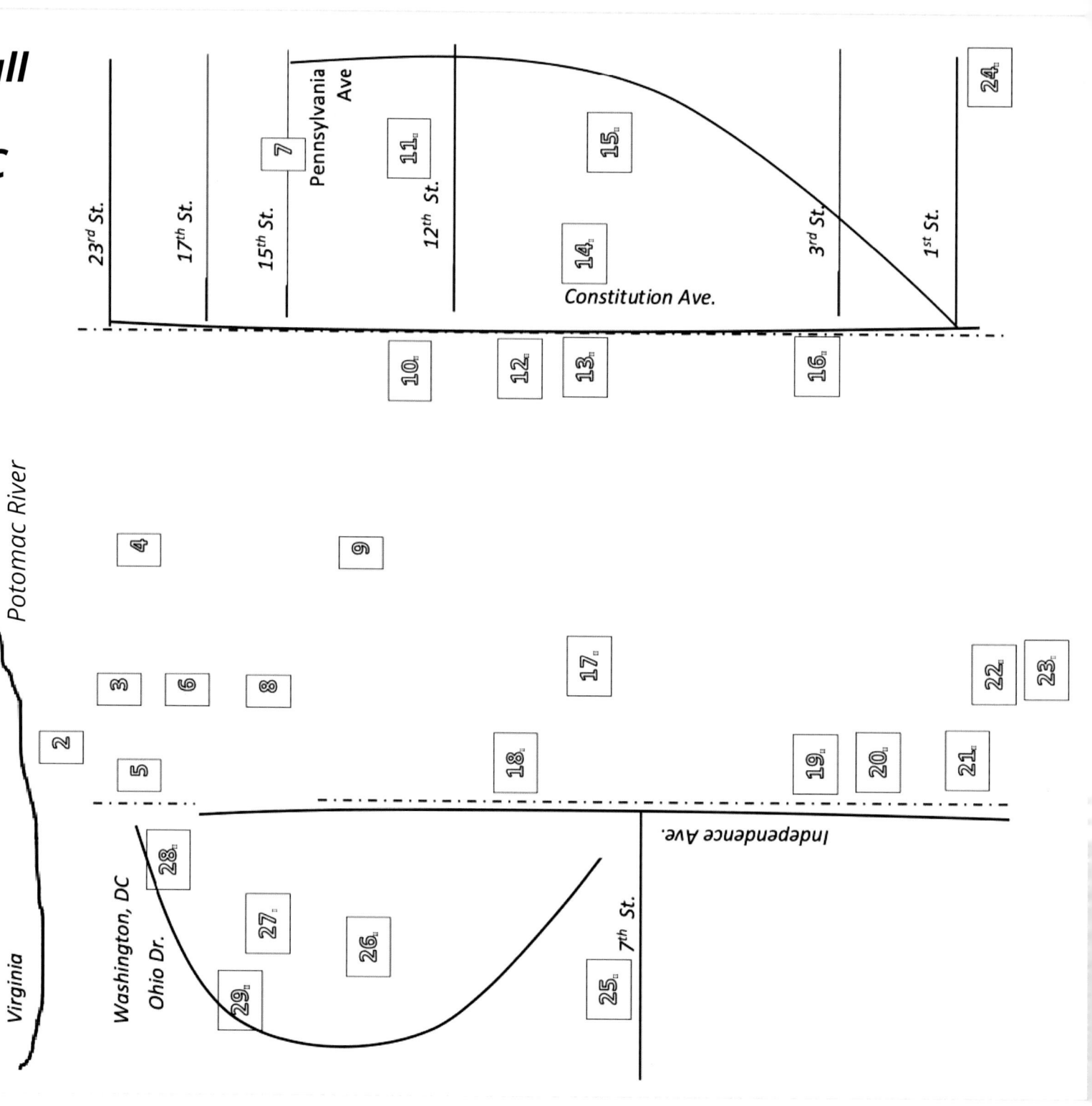

What's on The Map

1. Arlington National Cemetery
2. Memorial Bridge
3. Lincoln Memorial
4. Vietnam Memorial
5. Korean War Veteran's Memorial
6. National World War II Memorial
7. The White House
8. Washington Monument
9. National Museum of African American History and Culture
10. National Museum of American History
11. National Children's Museum
12. National Museum of Natural History
13. National Gallery of Art Sculpture Garden
14. National Archives Building
15. National Portrait Gallery
16. National Gallery of Art
17. Carousel on the Mall
18. Smithsonian 'castle' (Smithsonian Institution Building)
19. National Air and Space Museum
20. National Museum of the American Indian
21. U.S. Botanic Garden
22. United States Capitol
23. Library of Congress
24. National Postal Museum
25. International Spy Museum
26. Jefferson Memorial
27. Tidal Basin
28. MLK (Martin Luther King) Memorial
29. FDR (Franklin Delano Roosevelt) Memorial

The National Mall - - - - - - - - - - - - - - -

Note: Most streets do not appear on the map.

Fun Facts about Washington DC Sites

Draw a line from the fact on the left to the correct site on the right

Facts Sites

Years ago, the land at this site was a village where slaves going to freedom could get housing, education, and medical care.

You may have seen pictures of this site before – it appears on the back of the five-dollar bill. Ask your parents to show you.

The statues in this site are constructed to make you feel that at least one is looking at you wherever you stand.

There are 4,048 gold stars around this memorial! – one for every 100 American soldiers who lost their lives in the war.

When it was completed in 1884, this was the tallest building in the world (more than 555 feet tall)! Now there are lots of taller buildings. How many feet taller is it than you?

There are more than 1.8 million objects here that help tell the story of America's history.

Sites:
- National Museum of American History
- Korean War Veterans Memorial
- National World War II Memorial
- The Lincoln Memorial
- Washington Monument
- Arlington National Cemetery

Fun Facts cont.

Facts ### **_Sites_**

Facts	Sites
This museum calls its interactive experience for children STEAM (science, technology, engineering, arts, and math).	National Museum of the American Indian
This museum has 145 million live specimens and artifacts showing the history of Earth and helping humans understand the world and their place in it.	U.S. Capitol
The panels on the exterior of this museum are designed to be just like a crown on the head of a statue inside the museum.	National Air and Space Museum
More than 311 million people have visited this museum since it opened in 1976.	National Museum of African American History and Culture
As of 2020, 9.2 million Americans describe themselves as having their ancestry honored through this museum.	National Children's Museum
In all, there are 100 statues of famous American figures -- two provided by each of the 50 U.S. states – in and around Statuary Hall, one of the most popular rooms in this building.	National Museum of Natural History

Fun Facts about Washington DC Sites - ANSWERS

Facts

Years ago, the land at this site was a village where slaves going to freedom could get housing, education, and medical care.

You may have seen pictures of this site before – it appears on the back of the five-dollar bill. Ask your parents to show you.

The statues on this site are constructed to make you feel that at least one is looking at you wherever you stand.

There are 4,048 gold stars around this memorial – one for every 100 American soldiers who lost their lives in the war.

When it was completed in 1884, this was the tallest building in the world (more than 555 feet tall)! Now there are lots of taller buildings. How many feet taller is it than you?

There are more than 1.8 million objects here that help tell the story of America's history.

Sites

National Museum of American History

Korean War Veterans Memorial

National World War II Memorial

The Lincoln Memorial

Washington Monument

Arlington National Cemetery

Fun Facts cont. - ANSWERS

Facts

This museum calls its interactive experience for children STEAM (science, technology, engineering, arts, and math).

This museum has 145 million live specimens and artifacts showing the history of Earth and helping humans understand the world and their place in it.

The panels on the exterior of this museum are designed to be just like a crown on the head of a statue inside the museum. Ask your parents if you can touch one!

More than 311 million people have visited this museum since it opened in 1976.

As of 2020, 9.2 million Americans describe themselves as having their ancestry honored through this museum.

In all, there are 100 statues of famous American figures -- two provided by each of the 50 U.S. states – in and around Statuary Hall, one of the most popular rooms in this building.

Sites

National Museum of the American Indian

U.S. Capitol

National Air and Space Museum

National Museum of African American History and Culture

National Children's Museum

National Museum of Natural History

Scavenger Hunt

Find each picture of the below things in the pages of this book or find each of the below things in Washington DC

1. Carousel on the National Mall
2. Stamp of Owney the U.S. Postal Service dog at the National Postal Museum
3. Dingo at the National Museum of Natural History
4. Ducks in the Capitol Hill reflecting pool
5. Fala at the FDR Memorial
6. Giant spider at the National Gallery of Art Sculpture Garden
7. Giant whale hanging on the ceiling of the National Museum of Natural History
8. Head of a Bull (by Gaetano Monti)
9. Horses in the painting of Battle of Little Big Horn, National Museum of the American Indian
10. Jaguar at the Library of Congress
11. Man and dog crossing country in an old-time car, National Museum of American History
12. Sydney, the first dog to go to Antarctica, National Air and Space Museum
13. The words of Abraham Lincoln's Gettysburg Address
14. Soldiers at the Korean War Memorial
15. Yawning Tiger, National Gallery of Art (by Anna Hyatt Huntington)

Scavenger Hunt - ANSWERS

1. Carousel on the National Mall, page 20
2. Stamp of Owney the U.S. Postal Service dog at the National Postal Museum, page 27
3. Dingo at the National Museum of Natural History, page 19
4. Ducks in the Capitol Hill reflecting pool, page 25
5. Fala at the FDR Memorial, page 29
6. Giant spider at the National Gallery of Art Sculpture Garden, page 17
7. Giant whale hanging on the ceiling of National Museum of Natural History, page 18
8. Head of a Bull (by Gaetano Monti), page 21
9. Horses in the painting of Battle of Little Big Horn, National Museum of the American Indian, page 24
10. Jaguar at Library of Congress, page 26
11. Man and dog crossing country in an old-time car, National Museum of American History, page 15
12. Sydney, the first dog to go to Antarctica, National Air and Space Museum, page 22
13. The words of Abraham Lincoln's Gettysburg Address, page 10
14. Soldiers at the Korean War Memorial, page 11
15. Yawning Tiger, National Gallery of Art (by Anna Hyatt Huntington), page 21

Word Search (look left-to-right, up-to-down, and diagonal)

```
S S G B O T A N I C R Y I C H S V S G J
S O Y G C O J J O I A T V A T H R U W O
H K M K S N M E X U F M V C E L I M L D
V I E E N N O F F L J R X E Q P U T W O
J Y T Q Y S N F A R A D G B P R E P A W
B P R Z P T U E L U R S G R A P M F S N
E P O B A D M R A N O R M J D K L B H E
L V M M R O E S O H I O H K D X V B I Y
Z M C F T G N O L C O C U O L C H T N W
N E X F I B T N X H J K S R E S N Y G V
S M G A F W U D Y A D E I E X D I F T X
P O W U A S X K A W G T Y A V S X D O G
K R K R C U U F E P X I J N T A M V N L
X I C T T H N Y K O K K A J W J I J A I
P A J Z B O X Q X S P I G C E J P P K B
N L D Z G B F O V T H M S C T I D A L R
A V M H U R C D J A K U O O H F W G R A
P A L I N C O L N L H G M S S V Q U G R
D O G S M Y C C C P V G E A Y P R G Z Y
F N Z C A P I T O L O X E G N W K C J L
```

1. Artifact
2. Washington
3. Owney
4. Memorial
5. Capitol
6. Botanic
7. Lincoln
8. Jefferson
9. Paddle
10. Tidal
11. Dogs
12. Rocket
13. Human
14. Nap
15. Monument
16. Korean
17. Library
18. Postal
19. Fala
20. Metro

Add extra words you find here: _____ _____ _____
_____ _____ _____

Word Search - ANSWERS

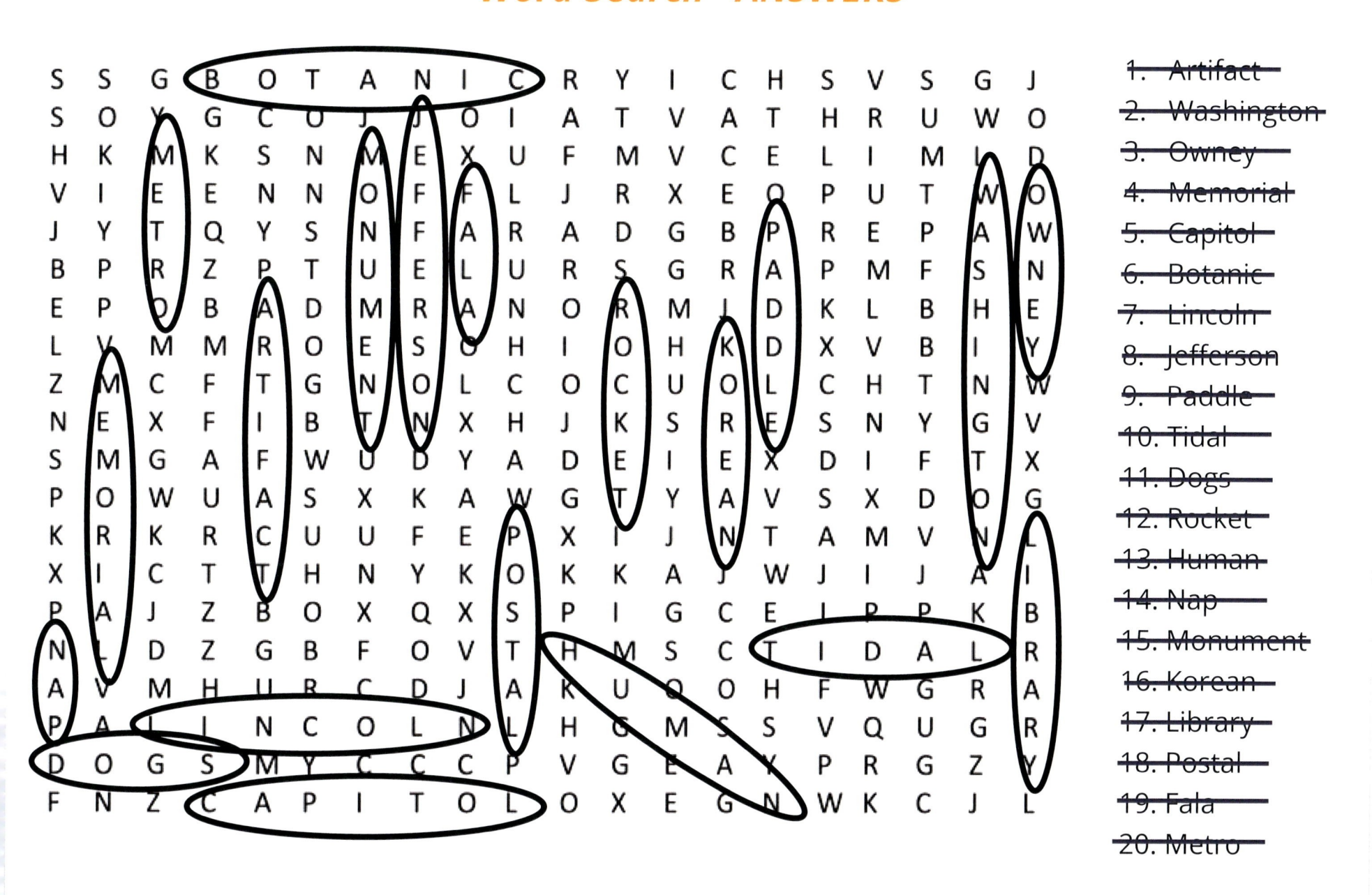

1. Artifact
2. Washington
3. Owney
4. Memorial
5. Capitol
6. Botanic
7. Lincoln
8. Jefferson
9. Paddle
10. Tidal
11. Dogs
12. Rocket
13. Human
14. Nap
15. Monument
16. Korean
17. Library
18. Postal
19. Fala
20. Metro

What Else to See When You Rocket around DC

Check each one you would like to see!

___Ride the paddle boats on the Tidal Basin
___African American Civil War Memorial
___Bureau of Engraving and Printing
___Chinatown
___DC United men's soccer game
___DC Waterfront (District Wharf)
___DC World War I Memorial
___Eastern Market
___Eisenhower Memorial
___Emancipation Memorial
___Freedom Plaza
___Food and ice cream from the food trucks
___Ford's Theater
___Lockkeeper's House at Washington Monument
___Japanese American National Museum
___Hirshhorn Museum and Sculpture Gallery
___National Building Museum
___National Cathedral
___National Geographic Museum

National Shrine___
National Women's History Museum___
Smithsonian National Zoo___
The Corcoran Art Gallery___
The Folger___
The Shakespeare Theatre___
The Supreme Court___
The Willard Hotel___
Union Station___
US Navy War Memorial___
US National Arboretum___
Vietnam Women's Memorial___
Washington Capitals hockey game___
Washington Commanders football game (Maryland)___
Washington Mystics women's basketball game___
Washington Nationals baseball game___
Washington Spirit women's soccer game___
Washington Wizards men's basketball game___
US Holocaust Memorial Museum___

Be a Rocketarounder!

--Share Rocket's values of building your brain through adventure, imagination, and finding new ways to have fun!

--Read *Rocket Around Washington DC* AND do the activities

--Let Rocket's human family know: Where should Rocket and his humans go next? Where would your dog want to rocket around with Rocket? (make sure your mom or dad is okay with it first). Email your ideas to lee@rocketaround.com

If you did these things,
you are an official Rocketarounder -
welcome to the Club!

I'M A ROCKETAROUNDER!

I build my brain through:

-Adventure
-Imagination
-Finding new ways to have fun!

The Humans + Rocket

Rocket is real, and he lives with his awesome (his word, not ours) neurodiverse family in Alexandria, VA.

They love seeing new things, traveling, reading, writing, sports, music, chess, anime, chewing sticks and toys, and sleeping.

They hope you enjoyed this book and that you'll read the next one!